LGBTQ
Issues

Violence Against the LGBTQ Community

Hal Marcovitz

ReferencePoint
Press

San Diego, CA

© 2021 ReferencePoint Press, Inc.
Printed in the United States

For more information, contact:
ReferencePoint Press, Inc.
PO Box 27779
San Diego, CA 92198
www.ReferencePointPress.com

LIBRARY OF CONGRESS CATALOGING-IN-PUBLICATION DATA

Names: Marcovitz, Hal, author.
Title: Violence Against the LGBTQ Community / Hal Marcovitz.
Description: San Diego : ReferencePoint Press, 2020. | Series: LGBTQ issues |
Includes bibliographical references and index.
Identifiers: LCCN 2020024030 (print) | ISBN
  9781682829196 (library binding) | ISBN 9781682829202 (ebook)
Subjects: LCSH: Sexual minorities--United States--Juvenile literature. |
  violence--Legal status, laws, etc.--United States. | Human
  rights--United States--Juvenile literature. | Gay rights--United
  States--Juvenile literature.

Contents

The Very Real Dangers Facing the LGBTQ Community

The incident started out as a routine chapter in American life. Two cars were involved in a minor accident in a parking lot in Dallas, Texas. Such accidents happen dozens if not hundreds of times a day in big cities and small towns across America. Typically, when such accidents occur the two drivers resolve the matter amicably, exchanging information about their auto insurance companies, which then sort out the details and decide who is responsible for paying for the damages. But that is not how the incident on April 12, 2019, played out.

One of the drivers was Muhlaysia Booker, a twenty-three-year-old transgender woman—meaning she was born male but identifies as a woman. She adopted a woman's name, dresses as a woman, wears a woman's hairstyle and makeup, and when the law permits it, uses women's restrooms in public places like schools and restaurants. As the incident in Dallas unfolded, Booker exited her car, but as the other driver got out of his vehicle as well, he drew a gun on Booker and demanded she pay for the damages to his car immediately.

A crowd quickly surrounded the two. Antigay shouts and taunts rained down on Booker. And then a man, Edward Thomas, stepped out of the crowd and began assaulting Booker. As he flailed away at the hapless victim, members of the crowd cheered him on. Somebody in the crowd offered $200 to Thomas to keep assaulting Booker. And then others in the crowd joined in the fray, throwing punches and kicks at Booker as she lay helplessly on the asphalt parking lot. Finally, some women in the crowd stepped forward and pulled Booker to safety.

Rise in Crimes Against the LGBTQ Community

Booker suffered fractured bones in her face. In fact, it was not the first time she had been assaulted for no reason other than the fact that complete strangers felt uncomfortable in her presence and responded by physically assaulting her. Sadly, Booker's plight illustrates the circumstances under

A picture of transgender woman Muhlaysia Booker is held while her father speaks to people attending her vigil. A month after a minor car accident led to a brutal beating, Booker was found shot to death.

which many people known as LGBTQ—lesbian, gay, bisexual, transgender, and queer or questioning—are forced to live their lives in America and elsewhere. For many, the fear of being violently attacked follows them wherever they go. Says R.J. Parker, an author who has studied crimes against the LGBTQ community:

> The lesbian, gay, bisexual and transgender community has faced violence, hate and persecution for a very long time. Usually, the perpetrators of these . . . crimes are fanatics . . . who believe these people defy the [traditional heterosexual] gender roles and, hence, are not fit to be part of society. Various acts of violence involving assault, torture, harassment, and sometimes murder, have been carried out against members of the LGBT community.[1]

According to the FBI, hate crimes against the LGBTQ community rose by 6 percent from 2017 to 2018, the last years for which statistics are available. Hate crimes are crimes committed by perpetrators who harbor biases against their victims' race, ethnicity, faith, sexual preference, or gender identity. In 2018 there were a total of 1,196 hate crimes committed against members of the LGBTQ community, up from 1,130 the year before. Those statistics included an increase of 15 percent against members of the transgender community. There were 303 cases reported against transgender Americans in 2018, compared to 268 the year before. Alphonso David, president of the Human Rights Campaign, a Washington, DC–based civil rights organization, says:

> Bias-motivated crimes are a real, frightening problem in the United States, and LGBTQ people continue to be targeted because of who they are. In 2018, we know that at least 28 transgender people were violently killed. . . . These numbers represent real people—people with friends, families and lives. The epidemic of violence against LGBTQ people . . . is staggering, and it is something we must address head-on.[2]

Under Constant Threat

Following the assault on Booker, she became an outspoken advocate for the LGBTQ community in Dallas and elsewhere, speaking at rallies and other events aimed at raising awareness for the rights of LGBTQ people. "[The] time to seek justice is now," Booker said at an LGBTQ rally in Dallas a week after her assault. "This time, I can stand before you, where in other scenarios, we're at a memorial."[3]

Aided by cell phone video that recorded the attack on Booker, police in Dallas were soon able to make an arrest in the assault on the transgender woman. Thomas was charged in the assault, convicted by a jury, and sentenced to ten months in prison. But that is not where Booker's sad story ends. A month after Booker was assaulted in the parking lot, her body was found in a Dallas street, the victim of a gunshot wound.

"Bias-motivated crimes are a real, frightening problem in the United States, and LGBTQ people continue to be targeted because of who they are."[2]

—Alphonso David, president of the Human Rights Campaign

Police soon arrested a suspect, Kendrell Lavar Lyles, charging him with the murder of Booker. By early 2020 Lyles had not yet come to trial. Nor had police disclosed what they believed to have been a motive in the case—or whether Booker had once again been targeted for violence because she identified as a transgender woman. Still, the unfortunate course of Booker's life after she decided to live as a woman illustrates that all members of the LGBTQ community are under constant threat of physical violence simply for wanting to be themselves.

Chapter One

A History of Violence Against the LGBTQ Community

Violence and other forms of abuse against members of the LGBTQ community are not new developments in world culture. Members of the LGBTQ community have endured hate and abuse for centuries, dating as far back as 400 CE, when leaders of the Roman Empire declared homosexuality a crime punishable by death. Says University of Arizona literature professor Marilyn B. Skinner, "[An] imperial decree provided that male prostitutes from Roman brothels should be rounded up and burned alive. In 438 the punishment was extended to every man found to have allowed himself to be penetrated."[4]

Death penalties against gay people were enforced during the Middle Ages and as late as the nineteenth century in England. In 1533 the British Parliament passed a law known as the Buggery Act—*buggery* was a slang term for homosexual intercourse. The penalty was death, and it remained the law in Great Britain until 1861, when Parliament eased the penalty on homosexual behavior. Under the new Offences Against the Person Act, the penalty for engaging in a homosexual act in Great Britain was eased to ten years in prison.

If gay men and women did manage to avoid prison or the death penalty, they nevertheless found themselves outcasts from society. During World War II, an estimated ten thousand gay and lesbian Europeans died in Nazi concentration camps—they were rounded up and imprisoned for no other reason than the fact that they were gay. Today homosexuality is still regarded as a crime in at least seventy nations. And in thirteen countries, among them Iran and Saudi Arabia, the crime of homosexuality is punishable by death.

Homophobia

The beliefs that led to the order to execute homosexuals in ancient Rome, or send them to prisons or death camps in nineteenth- and twentieth-century Europe, can be largely attributed to a state of mind later termed *homophobia*: the hatred and prejudice harbored against members of the gay community. The term was first used in 1969 by psychologist George Weinberg as he

During World War II, an estimated ten thousand gay and lesbian Europeans died in Nazi concentration camps. Today homosexuality is still regarded as a crime in at least seventy nations.

looked for answers to why members of the LGBTQ community had so often been shunned and abused.

Weinberg said he witnessed how gay people he knew prompted revulsion among some heterosexuals, even among many of his friends who were otherwise well-educated university professors. "They always had reasons for avoiding these people," he says. "They weren't at all distressed by the worst kinds of brutalities toward gays. I realized that something else was going on—more than simple miseducation. This was some deep emotional misgiving these people had, some phobic dread. It seemed to me the problem was theirs, not the homosexual's."[5]

Weinberg labeled this mental condition homophobia. He came to believe that homophobia is deeply rooted in the human brain, a product of growing up and later living in an environment in which people are accustomed to shunning members of the gay community. Weinberg found many ways in which homophobia had been ingrained in society. Perhaps churchgoers were told from the pulpits that homosexuality is wrong—passages in the Old Testament and New Testament condemn homosexuality. Likewise, the sacred texts of Islam outlaw homosexuality—as evidenced by the death penalties still in place in Saudi Arabia, Iran, and other Islamic countries. Of all the major world religions, the Hindu faith is perhaps the most accepting of homosexuality—Hindu scholars find no edicts in their sacred texts specifically condemning homosexuality. And yet it was not until 2018 that the Supreme Court of India—the nation with the largest population of Hindus in the world, some 1.4 billion people—overturned a national law condemning homosexuality as a crime. It was a law first enacted for India by the country's British overlords in 1861, even remaining on the books for more than seventy years after the British had given up their claim to sovereignty over the Indian subcontinent.

Outside of churches, homophobia found its way into schools and workplaces as well as other corners of society. In 1934 the

> "This was some deep emotional misgiving these people had, some phobic dread."[5]
>
> —George Weinberg, psychologist

Assaults on the LGBTQ Community in Russia

Government leaders as well as many citizens are known to be outwardly hostile to members of the LGBTQ community in Russia. In recent years the mayors of many Russian cities have refused to grant permits to LGBTQ activists to stage pride movement parades. Said Yury Luzhkov, the former mayor of Moscow, "For several years, Moscow has experienced unprecedented pressure to conduct a gay pride parade, which cannot be called anything but a satanic act."

After Luzhkov stepped down as mayor in 2010, gay rights activists hoped to revive the idea of staging pride parades and similar events in Russian cities, but by 2020 their efforts remained stalled. An effort by the Russian gay rights group Resource LGBTQIA Moscow to stage a conference in 2018 was canceled on the day of the event after the venue that agreed to provide meeting space for the delegates received threats of violence from anonymous callers.

Moreover, when two delegates arrived for the conference, they were assaulted outside the venue by an unidentified man who sprayed them with pepper spray—a chemical compound that temporarily blinds one, typically used for self-defense. When police were summoned, they refused to investigate the incident. "It is totally unacceptable for activists to face threats and attacks simply for holding a conference," says Graeme Reid, director of the LGBTQ rights program for Human Rights Watch, a US–based international civil rights group. "The Russian authorities need to do more to ensure that these threats and attacks stop."

Quoted in Alex Marquardt, "Moscow Mayor Bans 'Satanic' Gay Parade," ABC News, January 26, 2010. https://abcnews.go.com.

Quoted in Human Rights Watch, "Russia: LGBT Conference Attacked, Disrupted," November 12, 2018. www.hrw.org.

Hays Code, which set standards for the content of Hollywood films, decreed that gay characters could not be portrayed on screen. In 1942, as the US military drafted millions of men to serve in the armed forces in World War II, military officials devised tests to help recruiters tell whether draftees or volunteers were gay—and if recruiters concluded they were, to reject them for military service. In 1949 California became the first state to outlaw the employment of gay teachers in public schools. In 1953 President Dwight D. Eisenhower signed an order excluding gay individuals from federal employment; within two years some fifteen hundred gay men and women had lost their federal jobs.

And so, people who grew up and entered adulthood in these atmospheres of prejudice would come to regard gay people with suspicion and fear. And they often passed these notions on to the generations that followed them, embedding in the minds of their children the belief that gay people are evil and not to be accepted into mainstream society. Writing in 1972, Weinberg noted:

> Despite massive evidence that homosexuals are as various in their personalities as anyone else, the public at this time still holds many misconceptions which in some cases are thought to justify our discriminatory practices. Among those misconceptions are the belief that homosexuals seduce young children (child molestation is preponderantly a heterosexual practice); the belief that homosexuals are untrustworthy; that homosexual men hate women; that homosexual women hate men—all beliefs unsupported by evidence, but held unquestionably by millions.[6]

The Stonewall Riots

If you were a gay person applying for a teaching job in the 1950s in a school district that would not hire gay people, it is unlikely that you would have admitted to being gay on your application. Similarly, if you applied for a job with the federal government, it is not likely you would have let it be known during your job interview that you were gay. And if you were the victim of what today is called a hate crime, it is not likely that after you summoned the police you would have admitted to the officer that you were gay.

Following World War II, violence against gay people was not believed to be a significant issue—largely because most gay people did not want it to be known that they were gay. Gay people were generally ostracized by society and even harassed by police. Therefore, if a gay man was assaulted, it is likely he either would not report the attack, or if he did, he would not tell police that he was gay. Says James Polchin, a New York University historian, "It's clear, I think, that gay men were targets because [perpetrators]

knew they could be robbed or assaulted with little consequences. Mostly because homosexuality was criminalized. So it put queer men in a more vulnerable position in the legal system."[7]

But that attitude changed in 1969. By then it was not unusual for gay men and women to be harassed by police for no reason other than the fact that police suspected them of being gay. To find comraderie and companionship, members of the LGBTQ community often congregated in so-called gay bars. They felt

In 1969 police raided a gay bar called the Stonewall Inn (pictured today) in New York City. The bar patrons stood up to the police and inspired thousands of gay citizens to protest in the streets of New York.

Homosexuality and the Death Penalty

Being a member of the LGBTQ community is regarded as a crime in about seventy countries, including thirteen nations where engaging in a sexual relationship with a member of one's own sex is punishable by death. In many of the other countries, such as Nigeria and Yemen, LGBTQ people can be punished by being publicly whipped or pelted with stones. In some countries, members of the LGBTQ community typically face years in prison.

The most recent known case of the death penalty being carried out against a gay individual was in Iran in 2019 when a man was hanged for committing the crime of homosexuality. The harsh penalty for homosexuality was instituted following Iran's 1979 revolution, which installed a fundamentalist Islamic regime in control of the government. In 2007, during a visit to Columbia University in New York City, then-Iranian president Mahmoud Ahmadinejad told an audience, "In Iran, we don't have homosexuals, like in your country."

Following the execution of the thirty-one-year-old defendant, Iranian writer and activist Shadi Amin (who now lives in Germany) said, "Humiliation, repression and sexual harassment of a particular social group should be viewed critically and prohibited by law. . . . LGBT rights are human rights. Iran must not violate them by giving religious or cultural reasons."

Quoted in Hristina Byrnes, "Thirteen Countries Where Being Gay Is Legally Punishable by Death," *USA Today*, June 14, 2019. www.usatoday.com.

Quoted in Alistair Walsh, "Iran Defends Execution of Gay People," DW, June 12, 2019. www.dw.com.

accepted and at home in these establishments—although they were often subjected to raids by police. On June 28, 1969, police raided the Stonewall Inn, a gay bar in New York, arresting thirteen people for allegedly violating an archaic city law that prohibited men from wearing women's clothes. Other patrons of the bar were ordered to disperse, but instead they fought back against the police. A riot ensued that lasted for six days as thousands of gay citizens protested in the streets of New York.

The Stonewall riots marked the beginning of a change in attitude by members of the LGBTQ community: Many were now willing to openly declare their sexual preferences. The Stonewall riots marked the birth of the pride movement. With the support of the movement, members of the LGBTQ community demanded the same protections and equal treatment that were then being granted to African Americans and other ethnic minorities, as well as women, who had campaigned for years for equal pay and abortion rights. As the riots occurred in 1969, the noted gay poet Allen Ginsberg said, "Gay power! Isn't that great! It's about time we did something to assert ourselves. You know, the guys there [at Stonewall] were so beautiful—they've lost that wounded look that [we] all had 10 years ago."[8]

> "Gay power! Isn't that great! It's about time we did something to assert ourselves."[8]
>
> —Allen Ginsberg, poet

Governments responded to the new activism by gay Americans by passing civil rights legislation prohibiting discrimination against members of the LGBTQ community, eventually including marriage equality laws that legalized same-sex marriage. Several political leaders, among them US representatives Barney Frank of Massachusetts and Tammy Baldwin of Wisconsin, acknowledged they were gay. In 2020 former South Bend, Indiana, mayor Pete Buttigieg was briefly a candidate for the US presidency. During the campaign, Buttigieg often spoke about his close relationship with his husband, Chasten Glezman.

The Assassination of Harvey Milk

But just because society is more accepting of LGBTQ people than it was decades ago does not mean they are shielded from violence. Homophobia is still very much a state of mind harbored by many Americans as well as citizens of other countries. Since most members of the LGBTQ community no longer hide their sexuality or gender identity, incidents of crimes against them are now regularly reported to police.

Perhaps the first significant crime committed against a gay American in the aftermath of the Stonewall riots was the 1978 assassination of Harvey Milk. Milk was a gay political leader in

San Francisco who was shot to death by a political rival, Dan White. Milk and White were both city supervisors; in 1978 Milk pushed through a city ordinance outlawing discrimination against gay people in employment, housing, and other segments of city society. "This will be the most stringent gay rights law in the country," said Milk. "This one has teeth; a person can go to court if his rights are violated once this is passed."[9] A single city supervisor, White, voted against the ordinance.

Nine months later White resigned his seat. Days later he returned to city hall and shot and killed Milk and George Moscone, the San Francisco mayor who signed Milk's gay rights ordinance into law. Charged with the murders of Milk and Moscone, White claimed during his trial that his addiction to junk food had skewed his thinking, causing him to kill Milk and Moscone. This so-called Twinkie defense found traction among jurors, who ultimately convicted White of the lesser offense of manslaughter.

White served five years in prison. The verdict and light sentencing of White touched off protests and rioting in San Francisco as police clashed with LGBTQ activists. Observers insisted it was not junk food that led to Milk's murder but rather White's homophobia.

Harvey Milk (left) and San Francisco mayor George Moscone sit together in the mayor's office during the signing of the city's gay rights bill. In 1978 the two were both shot and killed by former city supervisor and opponent of the bill Dan White.

"Harvey Milk died because he was a gay man," Milk's friend and journalist Wayne Friday said shortly after Milk was killed. "George Moscone died because he was a friend of gay people—they can never convince me otherwise, and I will go to bed every night praying that their killer pays the full price."[10] As for White, he took his own life two years after his release from prison.

Nightclub Shootings

In securing the relatively light sentence for White, his lawyers convinced jurors that homophobia was not the motivating factor in his decision to take the lives of Milk and Moscone. But in the case of the shooting at the Backstreet Cafe in Roanoke, Virginia, the assailant was very clear in his motivation to commit a crime that killed one victim and wounded six others: homophobia.

The Backstreet Cafe was a gay bar in Roanoke. On September 22, 2000, the assailant, Ronald Gay, walked into the bar and opened fire. Gay left the bar, dropped the gun onto a sidewalk, walked a few blocks, and then entered another bar, where he sat down and ordered a beer. Police soon caught up with Gay and took him into custody. "He was just swinging his arm and people were going down and dropping," said Anna Sparks, who had stopped into the bar with her partner to celebrate Sparks's birthday. "He was staring at me like he was saying, 'You are next.'"[11] Ultimately, though, Sparks was spared.

> "He was just swinging his arm and people were going down and dropping. He was staring at me like he was saying, 'You are next.'"[11]
>
> —Anna Sparks, survivor of the Backstreet Cafe shooting

When investigators spoke with Gay, he told them he had been taunted for years by friends and strangers who jokingly declared him to be gay because of his last name. Gay found he could no longer endure the jokes and decided to lash out at the LGBTQ community. He pleaded guilty to the Backstreet Cafe shooting and was sentenced to life imprisonment.

Homophobia was also the suspected motive in the murders of LGBTQ people at Pulse, a gay nightclub in Orlando, Florida, which in 2016 was the scene of a mass shooting in which forty-nine people were murdered with another fifty-three sustaining gunshot wounds. The perpetrator was Omar Mateen, who is believed to have been gay. Mateen was killed in a shootout with police the night of the murders. Mateen was a follower of fundamentalist Islam, which has outlawed homosexuality—which is punishable by death in nations governed under a strict interpretation of Islamic law. Therefore, it is believed that Mateen suffered from severe mental anguish—torn between his sexual orientation and his religious beliefs, he lashed out against the LGBTQ community.

The notion that gay people may themselves be homophobic was raised by Weinberg, who found such cases to be a genuine source of hatred directed toward gay people. Individuals, he said, may discover they are attracted to people of their own sex, and because of their antigay upbringings and beliefs, they may find it difficult to accept the truth about themselves. Wrote Weinberg, one "motive for the homophobic reaction is the fear of being homosexual oneself."[12]

Abuse on a Daily Basis

The homophobia expressed by White, Gay, and Mateen led to major crimes that dominated headlines and news broadcasts. But members of the LGBTQ community are confronted with abuse on a daily basis—and often such cases just seem to be part of normal life for gay people. Doug Meyer, an instructor in LGBTQ studies at the University of Virginia, described a typical case he encountered: Two women, Latoya and Brianna, were walking hand in hand on a New York City street. A man approached the two women and asked Brianna for her phone number, indicating he wanted to call her for a date. The two women tried to ignore the man, but he persisted. Finally, Latoya told the man, "Listen, she's not interested, she's with me."[13]

The man reacted by grasping Brianna's arm and shoving her to the ground. As Latoya ran to her partner, the assailant stormed off, shouting profanities at the two women. Says Meyer, "Latoya's

. . . experiences reveal that some forms of violence occur because of prejudice and discrimination . . . often referred to as homophobia. Indeed, it is possible—likely even—that Latoya and [Brianna] would not have experienced violence had they been heterosexual. The man in . . . the incident became upset when a lesbian woman said that her girlfriend was not interested in him."[14]

Violence against members of the LGBTQ community is likely to have started in ancient times, when leaders of the Roman Empire decreed homosexuality a crime punishable by death. Only in the last few decades of the twentieth century have members of the LGBTQ community made strides in winning the same rights afforded to all people in America and elsewhere. Yet the actions by perpetrators like White, Gay, Mateen, and the man who accosted Latoya and Brianna illustrate how LGBTQ individuals still very much face the threat of violence in their everyday lives.

Chapter Two

Internet Threats

For years, Jordan Steffy endured taunts and bullying from his classmates. Steffy, an eleventh-grade student at LaPorte High School in Indiana, came out as gay in the seventh grade. Since then, classmates had leveled homophobic insults at him, both to his face and online. He had learned to ignore the insults, but in 2019 one of his classmates posted a particularly vulgar message directed toward Steffy on Snapchat.

Later, when Steffy saw the student in class, he approached him. "He made an anti-gay post with a picture of me on it saying how he hated gays and a bunch of throwing up emojis all over it," Steffy says. "I walked up to him and said 'Why did you post this?' He said, 'It was just a post.' And I said, 'Well, it's not just a post. It's a post about me, saying how you dislike who I am, and I don't appreciate that.'"[15]

The confrontation soon escalated into physical violence between the two students. Classmates who witnessed the tussle made videos of the fight and posted them online. The incident lasted for about thirty seconds, until it was broken up by a teacher. In the end, both Steffy and his antagonist were suspended from school. Later, Steffy said he has no regrets about confronting his bully.

"I said, 'Well, it's not just a post. It's a post about me, saying how you dislike who I am, and I don't appreciate that.'"[15]

—Jordan Steffy, student at LaPorte High School in Indiana

"I just got sick of it," Steffy says. "It's crazy the amount of hatred I received just for liking who I like and being me."[16]

Bullied Online

The video displaying how Steffy stood up for himself earned the teen plaudits from national leaders in the LGBTQ movement. Says Melanie Willingham-Jaggers, deputy executive director of GLSEN, an LGBTQ education advocacy organization, "While we don't condone violence, it reflects the trauma that LGBTQ youth have endured and the fact that they feel they need to fend for themselves in school. Jordan deserves better. All students deserve better."[17]

The incident that sparked the confrontation between Steffy and his classmate reflects a very real danger to LGBTQ people: cyberbullying. Research has shown an overwhelming number of young people who identify as LGBTQ have been bullied online by

Research has shown an overwhelming number of young people who identify as LGBTQ have been bullied online by homophobic antagonists. And it appears incidents of cyberbullying are on the rise.

homophobic antagonists. A 2020 study by Iowa State University queried 350 members of the LGBTQ community aged eleven to twenty-two and determined that 54 percent of the respondents had been victims of cyberbullying. And it appears incidents of cyberbullying against young LGBTQ people are on the rise. In a 2013 study conducted by GLSEN, 42 percent of LGBTQ young people said they had experienced cyberbullying.

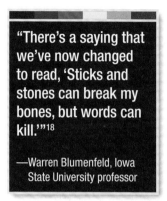

"There's a saying that we've now changed to read, 'Sticks and stones can break my bones, but words can kill.'"[18]

—Warren Blumenfeld, Iowa State University professor

Moreover, GLSEN reported that cyberbullying of LGBTQ youth is three times higher than cyberbullying experienced by other students. GLSEN also reported that 33 percent of gay students report sexual harassment online, 27 percent do not feel safe online, and 20 percent report receiving harassing text messages from other students. Says Warren Blumenfeld, a professor of curriculum and instruction at Iowa State University:

> There's a saying that we've now changed to read, "Sticks and stones can break my bones, but words can kill." And especially at this age—pre-adolescence through adolescence—this is a time when peer influences are paramount in a young person's life. If one is ostracized and attacked, that can have devastating consequences— not only physically, but on their emotional health for the rest of their lives.[18]

A typical case that illustrates how the internet is used to threaten LGBTQ students occurred in Utah in 2019. A video posted on Snapchat showed two players from the Kearns High School football team burning a gay pride flag and threatening to kill members of the school's LGBTQ community. Soon after the video was posted on social media, the two players were suspended from school. "There's no place for that in our program at all, and it won't be tolerated," said Kearns High School football coach Matt Rickards. "It sickens me."[19]

Anonymous Taunts and Insults

The issue of cyberbullying in the LGBTQ community first came to national attention with the 2010 case of Tyler Clementi, a student at Rutgers University in New Jersey who was videotaped, without his knowledge, kissing another gay student in his dorm room. The video was made with a hidden camera by Clementi's roommate,

How Predators Abuse Dating Apps

The British cybersecurity firm Pen Test Partners looked at dating apps developed for LGBTQ people and found several apps—among them Grindr, Recon, and Romeo—containing design flaws that allow predators to track the locations of users. Many of the apps enable predators to find the general location of users within a few hundred feet—similar to how the Amazon app tells buyers the location of an approaching delivery truck. But Pen Test Partners found that some minor manipulations of the dating apps can give predators the exact locations of users. The BBC reports:

Imagine a man shows up on a dating app as "200m away." You can draw a 200m (650ft) radius around your own location on a map and know he is somewhere on the edge of that circle. If you then move down the road and the same man shows up as 350m away, and you move again and he is 100m away, you can then draw all of these circles on the map at the same time and where they intersect will reveal exactly where the man is.

Says journalist Michael Grothaus, "Immediate thoughts of how a stalker could use this technique spring to mind, but that isn't the only worry. Homosexuality is illegal or socially unacceptable in many of the countries where gay men use Grindr, Recon, and Romeo. This method would allow a nation-state to easily track them down in real time, leaving their freedom and perhaps even lives at risk."

Michael Grothaus, "Gay Dating Apps Grindr and Romeo Can Expose User Locations, Leaving Men Vulnerable to Hate Crimes," *Fast Company*, August 8, 2019. www.fastcompany.com.

Dharun Ravi, then posted on Twitter. In his Twitter post, Ravi said, "Roommate asked for the room till midnight. I went into molly's room and turned on my webcam. I saw him making out with a dude. Yay."[20] Distraught over the video, Clementi jumped to his death from the George Washington Bridge that connects New Jersey with New York. Ravi was eventually criminally charged with invading Clementi's privacy; he served twenty days in jail.

Cyberbullying in Canada

Young members of the LGBTQ community in Canada are twice as likely to have been cyberbullied or cyberstalked as other internet users in that country, according to a study by Statistics Canada, the agency that analyzes life and culture in Canada. The study reports, "The proportion of those who experienced online victimization is greater for the homosexual and bisexual population. In this particular group, more than one-third (34 percent) reported that they had experienced cyberbullying, cyberstalking, or both, compared with 15 percent of the heterosexual population." The study looked at Canadians in the fifteen- to twenty-nine-year-old age group.

The study illustrates that cyberbullying and cyberstalking remain a problem in Canada even though Canadian provincial governments toughened their laws against bullying following the 2011 suicide of Jamie Hubley, a gay student at Jackson Secondary School in Kanata, Ontario. Hubley had endured cyberbullying for many years. "He just wanted someone to love him. That's all," says Jamie's father, Allan Hubley. "And what's wrong with that? Why do people have to be cruel to our children when all they want to do is be loved?"

In Ontario the provincial government passed the Accepting Schools Act. In addition to providing disciplinary measures for students found to be bullying online or in the schoolyard, the law requires schools to recognize the rights of LGBTQ students and encourage the establishment of gay-straight alliance (GSA) clubs on school campuses. GSA clubs work to develop ways LGBTQ students can find acceptance in schools.

Darcy Hango, "Cyberbullying and Cyberstalking Among Internet Users Aged 15 to 29 in Canada," Statistics Canada, December 19, 2016. www150.statcan.gc.ca.

Quoted in Chris Mikula, "Ottawa to Launch National Anti-bullying Program in Wake of 15-Year-Old Jamie Hubley's Suicide," *Toronto National Post*, June 2, 2013. https://nationalpost.com.

In the Clementi and Steffy cases, the victims were able to identify their bullies, but this is often not possible. Most cyberbullies post their taunts and insults anonymously, often using phony social media profiles.

Moreover, cyberbullies make it easy for others to join in the bullying. An insulting post placed on a social media site can be seen by anyone with internet access—literally billions of people. Not only does such extensive access to these bullying messages expose the victim to widespread ridicule, but others may view these posts as opportunities to join in the bullying. Making matters worse, a cyberbully can keep the pressure on a victim by sending texts to the victim's phone. Citing research published by the *Journal of Adolescent Health*, journalist Tara Parker-Pope notes:

> Although the majority of kids who are harassed online aren't physically bothered in person, the cyberbully still takes a heavy emotional toll on his or her victims. Kids who are tormented online are more likely to get a detention or be suspended, skip school and experience emotional distress. . . . Teens who receive rude or nasty comments via text messages are six times more likely to say they feel unsafe at school.[21]

"Although the majority of kids who are harassed online aren't physically bothered in person, the cyberbully still takes a heavy emotional toll on his or her victims."[21]

—Tara Parker-Pope, journalist

Suicide and Cyberbullying

Cyberbullying often has consequences that go far beyond serving a school suspension, particularly for members of the LGBTQ community. Many young members of the LGBTQ community have reacted to cyberbullying by taking their own lives. Channing Smith, a sixteen-year-old gay teen from Tennessee, took his own life in 2019 after he was harassed online. Text messages that Smith had been sharing with another gay boy were found by Smith's former girlfriend and posted on Instagram and Twitter.

Numerous students from Smith's school shared the posts, many offering vicious comments about Smith's sexuality. "It just breaks my heart that people found out and made fun of him for it," says Faith Honea, a friend and classmate of Smith. "The people who exposed him had absolutely no right. They made fun of him, hurt him and above all made him feel alone."[22]

John Ayers, a professor at San Diego State University in California and author of a 2017 study on teen suicide, says it is difficult to pinpoint specific causes for why young members of the LGBTQ community may take their own lives, but cyberbullying is definitely a factor. When young people are suicidal, he says, "and then they're exposed to a trigger, that final trigger can push them over the edge. The stressors that they face may be pushing them over the edge and making them act on that more."[23]

Moreover, young people feeling stress from cyberbullying may be in more danger of taking their own lives than adults are. They may not realize that help—such as psychological counseling to ease their own mental traumas or legal help to respond to the bullying, is available. John Ackerman, a psychologist at the Center for Suicide Prevention and Research at Nationwide Children's Hospital in Columbus, Ohio, says young people feel "like they can't control their world, and other people will not respond to them in a positive way. Being younger, they don't know that that will change."[24]

Cyberstalking

Cyberbullying is not the only internet threat facing LGBTQ individuals. Online dating sites and apps have become a popular tool for meeting romantic partners. About 30 percent of all US adults have used a dating website or app, according to a 2020 Pew Research Center report. Use of these sites and apps is even more widespread among lesbian, gay, and bisexual adults than among straight adults. When asked whether they had ever used a dating site or app, 55 percent of LGBTQ adults and 28 percent of straight adults said they had. Websites and dating apps designed

#1 in dates,
relationships and marriages

I am a: Woman ▾   Seeking a: Man ▾

Between ages: 25 ▾ and 35 ▾

Near ZIP/Postal code: Zipcode

View Photos »

Online dating sites have become a popular tool for meeting romantic partners. Use of these sites is even more widespread among lesbian, gay, and bisexual adults than among straight adults.

to enable members of the LGBTQ community to make connections and meet one another can lead to long-lasting, loving relationships. However, these sites have also been known to expose participants to danger.

Young people, who hope to bond with new sympathetic friends or experience romantic relationships, are particularly vulnerable to problem encounters when they connect with strangers online. Setting up in-person meetings is especially risky for unsophisticated teens, who do not always realize that their online contacts might not be who they say they are.

Young people in this position sometimes become victims of cyberstalking. This is the use of the internet by predators to find unsuspecting LGBTQ people and then subject them to physical abuse and other crimes, such as theft. A 2013 GLSEN report says, "LGBT and boys that question their sexual identity are more likely to be targeted by Internet offenders. Teens have been physically attacked when meeting up with someone they have met online. In most cases, the stranger attempted to portray themselves as interested in having a relationship or sex, then abused their target when they show up."[25]

Adults have had similar experiences when they attempted to meet up with other LGBTQ people through online communities. In 2018 police charged four men in Texas with assault and robbery after they posed as gay on the Grindr app, then manipulated victims into divulging their home addresses. The assailants, whose ages ranged from nineteen to twenty-one, were sentenced to ten to twenty years in prison for breaking into victims' homes, tying them up, and physically assaulting them. During the ordeals, the victims reported the perpetrators shouted gay slurs at them. "This case highlights the danger of the Internet and specifically, online apps," Texas federal prosecutor Joseph D. Brown said after the completion of one trial. "In this case, the defendants misused the Internet for sinister purposes in order to target an innocent man based on his sexual orientation, causing him bodily harm and damage to his property."[26]

The victims of the Texas robberies and assaults survived their ordeals, but that was not the outcome in a 2019 case in Detroit, Michigan. In this case thirty-one-year-old Brian Anderson was robbed and murdered by an alleged cyberstalker after arranging a meeting through the Grindr dating app. According to police, Anderson was shot and robbed by Demetris Nelson, who had portrayed himself as a gay individual on the dating app. Moreover, police said, Anderson was not Nelson's only victim. Nelson had often portrayed a gay man on the app so he could specifically target and rob gay victims. In addition to killing Anderson, Nelson was also charged with shooting, robbing, and wounding another gay man, twenty-six-year-old Malcolm Drake. "The allegations are that social media contacts were used to target, contact, rob, fatally shoot one gay man and seriously wound an-

Demetris Nelson (pictured) often portrayed himself as a gay individual on the dating site Grindr so he could target and rob gay victims. In 2019 Nelson is alleged to have robbed and murdered Brian Anderson.

other gay man,"[27] says Wayne County prosecutor Kym Worthy. By 2020 Nelson had not yet come to trial.

Privacy Is Uniquely Important

Legal experts warn of other dangers to LGBTQ individuals who use online dating websites and apps. They point out that digital information is routinely hacked and then made available on the internet. Since many members of the LGBTQ community value their privacy, by using the internet as a form of communication, they run the risk of their identities being made public. In fact, a 2019 study published in the journal *Law & Social Inquiry* reported that 15 percent of LGBTQ people who used dating apps found information about themselves reposted on internet sites without their permission. This can lead to cyberbullying or attacks by homophobic predators. Says Ari Ezra Waldman, a professor of law at New York University:

> Privacy over our sexual selves protects our dignity and autonomy. It allows us to speak our minds and maintain social relationships. But for queer people, privacy is uniquely important. . . . Privacy can also make us safer, especially with anti-queer hate crimes increasing. Privacy lets us both "come out" in our own time and, once we do, live our best lives out and proud. . . .
>
> The frequency with which queer people using social media, generally, and mobile dating apps, in particular, amplifies the privacy concerns we face compared with the general population. All digital dating platforms require significant disclosure. Selfies and other personal information are the currencies on which someone decides whether to swipe right or left, or click a heart, or send a message.[28]

The internet dominates seemingly all facets of life in the twenty-first century. That holds true for straight as well as LGBTQ individuals. Despite the potential dangers, dating apps and social media continue to be a dominant feature of daily life. Indeed, a 2017 study conducted by Stanford University in California found that 65 percent of same-sex couples reported meeting their partners through online dating sites and apps. One of those couples includes Pete Buttigieg, the 2020 presidential candidate who met his husband, Chasten Glezman, through the Hinge dating app.

The internet poses a threat to members of the LGBTQ community. Some of them may be cyberbullied and forced to defend themselves,

"Privacy over our sexual selves protects our dignity and autonomy. It allows us to speak our minds and maintain social relationships."[28]

—Ari Ezra Waldman, New York University law professor

as Jordan Steffy reacted when he was cyberbullied. Or the cyberbullying may result in a much sadder ending, as it did for Tyler Clementi and Channing Smith. Or members of the LGBTQ community may find themselves the victims of predators whose intentions focus on the crimes of robbery and murder. But members of the LGBTQ community want only to be treated as equals with other members of society. Many members of the LGBTQ community look forward to the day when they can use the internet to chat and meet friends with the confidence that the internet will not be used to threaten, bully, or otherwise harm them.

Chapter Three

Targeted by Hate

The LGBTQ Center of Southern Nevada has long provided services to members of the gay community in Las Vegas and nearby towns. Since 1993 the center has provided health checkups for members of the LGBTQ community, including tests for sexually transmitted diseases. Free meeting rooms and offices are provided for numerous LGBTQ groups, including the Lambda Business Association, which assists small businesses owned by gay and lesbian people. Also, the Las Vegas chapter of the national group PFLAG maintains its headquarters at the center. PFLAG seeks to improve relations among LGBTQ people and their parents and other family members.

The LGBTQ Center was originally located in a cramped storefront. But over the years the center proved to be so popular that in 2013 the group moved into a larger space in downtown Las Vegas. "For so long, people were closeted," says Candice Nichols, executive director of the LGBTQ Center. "They didn't talk about being gay. Ownership of a new center is saying, 'We're here. We're part of your community, and look what we've built.'"[29]

On the morning of September 5, 2019, employees of the LGBTQ Center arrived to find an ugly greeting awaiting them. A vandal had painted graffiti on the exterior of the center, using crude slurs to describe members of the LGBTQ community. Surveillance video showed the perpetrator, an adult male wearing a black hoodie, using a can of spray paint to deface the exterior wall of the center. "We woke up today like any other day, but on this day we're met with a reminder as to why we are still needed," LGBTQ Center officials said in a statement. "Hatred will not stop us, it shows us more and more that we need to stand taller, shout louder and love harder."[30]

It was actually the second time that year the center had been victimized. In June 2019, on the fiftieth anniversary of the Stonewall riots, perpetrators set fire to trees on the grounds of the center. "I am saddened that the center was the victim of a hate crime yet again,"[31] says Joe Oddo Jr., president of the LGBTQ Center.

Hate Speech

Graffiti is a common sight found in virtually every city and town in America and in other countries as well. Someone caught tagging a wall—writing names, symbols, or other images—can be charged with committing vandalism. The charge is usually punishable by a fine. But if the vandal paints slurs targeting race, faith, ethnicity, sexual preference, or gender identity, the law may regard the act as a hate crime. Hate crimes are federal offenses

Painting on public property without permission is vandalism. If a vandal paints slurs targeting race, faith, ethnicity, sexual preference, or gender identity, the law may regard the act as a hate crime.

that carry significant penalties, including lengthy prison sentences. Moreover, many state legislatures have adopted their own hate crime laws. And those federal and state laws frequently regard hate speech as a hate crime.

The First Amendment to the US Constitution guarantees the right of free speech to Americans, but hate crime laws do not regard hate speech as constitutionally protected. Eric David Rosenberg, a Florida attorney and expert on First Amendment law, says:

> When a method for expressing views is chosen that is intentionally designed to cause damage to the listener, such expression has as its main purpose to hurt and humiliate, not to assert facts or values. Absent the goal of asserting facts or values, the underlying premise of the First Amendment—to allow and protect the free exchange of ideas—is not applicable. Therefore, the goal of the speaker, simply to harm his or her victim, does not warrant the protection afforded by the First Amendment.[32]

As illustrated in the case of the LGBTQ Center of Southern Nevada, hate speech can be expressed in the form of graffiti. Or it can by conveyed in other ways—such as notes tacked to bulletin boards in campus dormitories or placards stapled onto utility polls in city neighborhoods. Hate speech can also be posted online—homophobic social media posts as well as websites are common. Unlike cyberbullying, online hate speech does not necessarily target a single victim—often it targets a group, such as members of a religion, a race or ethnicity, or the LGBTQ community.

A recent example of hate speech surfacing on the internet occurred in 2020 when administrators of Facebook, YouTube, and Spotify removed videos posted by the Malaysian punk rock band Bunkface. The video portrayed the band performing a song that calls for the death of LGBTQ individuals. Contacted by reporters, band members said the song was intended to send a message to members of the LGBTQ community, expressing the band's distaste for the growing LGBTQ presence in Malaysia. In a statement, the band members said, "We're only making it clear that we do not support the movement that tries to push 'rights' for LGBT here in Malaysia."[33] Before the social media platforms took down the video, numerous Bunkface fans had posted homophobic comments supporting the band and the song—illustrating how online hate speech can gain traction and prompt others to express their own hateful comments.

> "We're only making it clear that we do not support the movement that tries to push 'rights' for LGBT here in Malaysia."[33]
>
> —Punk rock band Bunkface

Longer Penalties for Hate-Fueled Crimes

Anti-LGBTQ graffiti and homophobic rock videos can be deeply hurtful and can encourage other verbal attacks, but these are not the most serious hate crimes. People who commit crimes of assault against others solely because they harbor hate toward their targets' ethnicity, race, faith, sexual preference, or gender identity can be charged with committing hate crimes under a federal hate crime statute enacted in 2009. They can also be charged under many state hate crime laws. In the state-adopted hate crime laws, penalties for assault and similar crimes vary from state to state. Generally, though, in states that have adopted hate crime laws, an assault case motivated by hate carries a much stiffer penalty than an assault case that might escalate from an argument in a bar or some other venue. Assaults that do not fall under hate crime laws ordinarily result in a sentence of probation (meaning the perpetrator would serve no prison time). In contrast, an assault fueled by bias would result in a jail sentence.

As for the federal hate crimes statute, perpetrators motivated by bias who cause injuries to their victims face prison terms ranging from ten years to life. Says Christopher Heath Wellman, a professor of philosophy at Washington University in St. Louis, Missouri:

> Since we are especially aghast at bias crimes we should want to express our most solemn condemnation for those

who commit these crimes. The most natural way for us to do so, of course, is to impose stiffer penalties for hate crimes. . . . Given the implicit but clear messages of bias crimes, it is all the more important that society use criminal law to communicate forcefully the message of hatred not only does not come from all of us, but is a loathsome message which we as a society will not tolerate.[34]

The Shepard-Byrd Act

The 2009 federal law that established harsh penalties for hate-fueled crimes was prompted by two horrific cases of bias, one of which involved a member of the LGBTQ community. On the night of October 6, 1998, Matthew Shepard, a gay college student, met two men in a bar in Laramie, Wyoming. The two men, Aaron McKinney and Russell Henderson, told Shepard they were gay and offered to give the student a ride home. Instead, they drove him to

Russell Henderson (left) and Aaron McKinney make their first court appearance in 1998. Both men were sentenced to life imprisonment for the murder of Matthew Shepard, a gay college student.

a remote field near Laramie, where they pistol-whipped Shepard, robbed him, took his shoes, and tied him to a fence post, leaving him to die with a fractured skull. A day later, a bicyclist discovered Shepard—he was still alive but in a coma. Shepard died six days later in a Colorado hospital.

McKinney and Henderson were arrested the same night as the assault on Shepard. After leaving Shepard in the field, they returned to Laramie, where they picked a fight with two Latino men. Police broke up the fight but suspected that McKinney and Henderson were involved in a much more sinister crime. While inspecting McKinney's truck, they found a blood-stained gun as well as Shepard's shoes and his credit card. Eventually, Henderson pleaded guilty to the murder of Shepard, while McKinney was convicted after a trial by jury. Both men were sentenced to life imprisonment.

Following Shepard's murder, leaders of the LGBTQ rights community lobbied members of Congress to pass a law enacting stiff penalties for hate crimes. It took more than a decade after Shepard's murder, but in 2009 Congress passed the Shepard-Byrd Act of 2009. (The act was also named for James Byrd Jr., an African American man murdered in a racist attack in Texas in 1998.) Upon signing the law in 2009, President Barack Obama said, "Prosecutors will have new tools to work with states in order to prosecute to the fullest those who would perpetrate such crimes, because no one in America should ever be afraid to walk down the street holding the hands of the person they love."[35]

> "No one in America should ever be afraid to walk down the street holding the hands of the person they love."[35]
>
> —Barack Obama, former US president

Hate Remains a Threat to LGBTQ People

Despite the adoption of the Shepard-Byrd Act, as well as the enactment of similar measures in many US states, hate crimes against members of the LGBTQ community continue to occur. A typical case occurred at a New York City subway stop

When Speech Is Protected by the First Amendment

Students attending a class titled Introduction to LGBTQ Studies at the University of Louisville in Kentucky were greeted at the classroom door in February 2020 by a student handing out copies of a thirty-two-page pamphlet titled *God & Sexuality*. The pamphlet was clearly anti-LGBTQ in its message, suggesting that homosexuality violates religious principles. After the incident came to the attention of school administrators, they concluded that the student was within his rights to distribute the pamphlet and that its message was protected by the First Amendment.

Although the pamphlet urged members of the LGBTQ community to abandon homosexuality in favor of heterosexuality, it did not preach acts of violence against LGBTQ people. "The pamphlets he was distributing did not qualify as hate speech," says John Karman, director of media relations for the university. "He's expressing his First Amendment rights, and he's allowed to leave the literature."

Members of the campus LGBTQ community were still troubled by the university's decision to permit distribution of the pamphlet. Says Ashley-Shae Benton, a lesbian student at the university, "Today it could be propaganda, and tomorrow it could be violence."

Quoted in Greta Anderson, "Hand-Delivered Hate or Free Speech Exercise?," *Inside Higher Ed*, February 7, 2020. www.insidehighered.com.

in January 2020 when Serena Daniari, a transgender woman, was approached by Pablo Valle. Valle is alleged to have spoken to Daniari—who could not hear him because she was wearing headphones. She removed the headphones and asked him to repeat what he had just said to her. When Daniari spoke, Valle realized he was engaged in a conversation with a transgender woman. He became enraged. He is alleged to have spat at the victim and slapped her in the face. Police intervened and charged Valle with committing a hate crime against Daniari. "I think some people have misconceptions about trans people, that we're deceptive. But that couldn't be further from the truth," Daniari said after the incident. "At the end of the day, we just want to commute to work and see our friends and family without the threat of violence. We're just like every other New Yorker."[36] Valle was charged under New York State's hate crimes law; by mid-2020 he had not yet come to trial.

Other countries have also adopted hate crime laws, among them England. In 2019 Melania Geymonat and Christine Hannigan were sitting hand in hand on a London bus when they were suddenly pelted with coins by three teenage boys who shouted homophobic slurs at the women. Each woman's face was bloodied by the attack. Says Hannigan, "We were clearly together in a romantic sense, we were being affectionate. It is pretty intimidating being cornered and making homophobic comments. They wanted us to show them how lesbians have sex. They said 'show us' and I don't remember if it was on its own or part of a larger phrase but the words were said."[37] The three perpetrators were charged under England's hate crimes law. A seventeen-year-old defendant was sentenced to four months in a youth incarceration center. The other two defendants, both fifteen years old, were sentenced in a juvenile court, and their punishments were not publicly announced.

> "I think some people have misconceptions about trans people, that we're deceptive. But that couldn't be further from the truth."[36]
>
> —Serena Daniari, hate crime victim

Years Added to a Sentence

Crimes motivated by bias, whether they are low-level or more serious crimes, typically result in more severe penalties. Prosecutors in Vancouver, Washington, were seeking enhanced punishment for a hate crime that occurred in December 2019. David Bogdanov, age twenty-five, was charged in the murder of seventeen-year-old Nikki Kuhnhausen, a transgender youth. In addition to homicide, prosecutors also charged Bogdanov with committing a hate crime under Washington State's hate crimes law because they believed he strangled the teen after learning she was transgender.

Police found that Bogdanov and Kuhnhausen first communicated on Snapchat, then arranged a meeting. Police allege Bogdanov was seeking a sexual encounter with a woman the night he met Kuhnhausen but, upon learning that she was transgender, became enraged and killed her. Later, he hid the body in a remote area of Washington State. "I believe that David became enraged at the realization that he had engaged in sexual contact with a male whom he believed to be female and strangled Nikki to death,"[38] says Vancouver police officer Jason Mills, who investigated the death.

By mid-2020 Bogdanov had not yet come to trial. He remained in custody under $2 million bail. Washington State does not impose the death penalty in homicide cases, meaning that if Bogdanov is convicted, the maximum penalty he would face is life

David Bogdanov and Nikki Kuhnhausen first communicated on Snapchat, then arranged a meeting. After learning that seventeen-year-old Kuhnhausen was transgender, Bogdanov killed her.

The Gay and Trans Panic Defense

Some defendants charged with targeting members of the LGBTQ community have invoked what is known as the gay and trans panic defense. The defense is based on the assertion by the defendants that they believed they were meeting persons of the opposite sex for dates but, upon learning their dates were gay or transgender, found themselves so anguished that they lashed out—panicked—and struck the victims. That was the defense invoked by James Dixon, charged in the 2013 death of a transgender woman, Islan Nettles, in New York City. Upon learning that Nettles was male, Dixon admitted to punching the victim in the face. Dixon's blow proved to be fatal.

He pleaded guilty to manslaughter. Prosecutors urged Judge Daniel P. Conviser to sentence Dixon to seventeen years in prison, but Dixon testified that he was a victim of trans panic, meaning he felt duped and humiliated after learning Nettles was transgender. Conviser sentenced the defendant to twelve years in prison.

Since 2014 ten states—California, Illinois, Rhode Island, Nevada, Connecticut, Maine, New York, New Jersey, Washington, and Hawaii—have outlawed the gay and trans panic defense, meaning defendants can no longer claim that personal anguish was the motivating factor in committing their crimes in those states. Seth Rosen, an attorney and director of development for the National LGBT Bar Association, has urged lawmakers in the other forty states to also ban the gay and trans panic defense. He says, "Lawmakers have to understand that this is a defense that devalues the lives of LGBTQ people."

Quoted in Juliette Maigné, "Trans Woman's Killer Used the 'Gay Panic Defense.' It's Still Legal in 42 States," Vice, July 21 2019. www.vice.com.

behind bars. Even if he does serve decades in prison, he could still conceivably become eligible for parole at some point and be released from jail. But under Washington State's hate crimes law, if Bogdanov is convicted and sentenced to a long prison term, he would not be eligible for release until he serves at least five additional years on the hate crimes charge.

Despite the adoption of hate crimes laws, hate crimes as well as hate speech represent a very real threat to the LGBTQ community. Sometimes these crimes can involve damage that can be repaired, such as the graffiti found on the walls of the LGBTQ Center in Las Vegas. But hate crimes can also inflict lasting damage, such as in the the deaths of innocent people such as Kuhnhausen and Shepard. This means that LGBTQ individuals must continue to be on guard against hate, because hate against members of the LGBTQ community remains an element of life in America and elsewhere.

Chapter Four

Pain and Anguish: The Effects of Violence

When Scott and Sharon Nelles woke up one morning in May 2019, they discovered dozens of plastic forks stuck into their front lawn. There was also a note staked to the lawn inscribed with the phone number of a suicide hotline. At first, the Nelleses did not know what to make of the incident. They believed it to be a harmless prank, similar to how teens may toss toilet paper at a house. But they soon concluded a hate crime had been committed against their family at their home in the Chicago, Illinois, suburb of Barrington. "Putting forks in someone's lawn can mean 'I hate you,' if you really hate somebody you say, 'Hey, let's go fork someone's lawn,'" says Scott. "In conjunction with . . . the suicide hotline number, we quickly realized this is something far more hateful."[39]

Moreover, it quickly became evident that the target of the hate crime was their daughter, a lesbian sophomore at Barrington High School. Sharon says her daughter had already been the victim of cyberbullying. She says that the lawn forking incident as well as the previous cyberbullying incidents have clearly caused her daughter to suffer mental stress. She explains, "She feels like there's a level of blame for her being gay and that was crushing to me. . . . When I look in her eyes, I feel sadness from her. I'm level-ten mad but she is just really worn out by it."[40]

High Rates of Suicide

As with the Nelleses' daughter, the targets of violence, hate speech, and other forms of abuse often experience mental anguish in the form of anxiety and depression. Anxiety and depression are both mental disorders. Anxiety is characterized by symptoms such as excessive worry or fear, inability to sleep, and restlessness. Symptoms of depression include feelings of sadness, lack of energy and appetite, inability to concentrate, and low self-esteem. According to the Centers for Disease Control and Prevention (CDC), members of the LGBTQ community who are the victims of homophobia, bullying, violence, or other forms of rejection are six times more likely than others to report high levels of depression. Says author Jonathan Charlesworth, executive director of Educational Action Challenging Homophobia, a Bristol, England–based LGBTQ rights group:

> "She feels like there's a level of blame for her being gay and that was crushing to me. . . . When I look in her eyes, I feel sadness from her."[40]
>
> —Sharon Nelles, mother of a bullied gay daughter

Homophobia has a negative effect on the health and well-being of young people and of those around them. . . . Too many gay young people report feeling any number of negative emotions: anxious, stressed, worthless, ashamed, angry, isolated, fearful with feelings of incredible loneliness and a sense of abnormality. These emotions can lead to depression, self-harm, eating disorders or suicide attempts. It is well recognized that suicide and attempted-suicide are far more frequent in those young people who identify as gay than in the general youth population. The role of homophobic bullying in contributing to these negative emotions and mental health issues cannot be underestimated.[41]

44

As Charlesworth notes, high rates of suicide among members of the LGBTQ community are common. A study conducted among young members of the LGBTQ community in Chicago, Illinois, found that following an episode of violence, verbal harassment, bullying, or similar form of abuse, a member of the LGBTQ community is nearly three times more likely than others to self-harm or attempt suicide. In making their findings, the study's authors interviewed 250 members of the LGBTQ community between ages sixteen and twenty. Write the authors of the study, "We emphasize that the prevalences of mental disorders and suicidal behaviors in our sample are sufficiently high to warrant special attention to the needs of this population."[42]

Sad Story of a Twelve-Year-Old Victim

Not only are members of the LGBTQ community who feel abused by others more likely to attempt suicide, but statistics show they are more likely than others to make attempts at self-harm

Few Gay Men Use Condoms

Many gay men seek solace from violence and abuse by turning to casual and unprotected sex with strangers. Condoms are regarded as an effective method for avoiding sexually transmitted diseases, but a CDC study shows that few gay men use them. In that study, which surveyed 9,640 gay men in twenty American cities, 65 percent of the respondents reported having had unprotected sex in the previous year. Moreover, the CDC report says that 37 percent of the respondents reported that they did not routinely use condoms with casual sex partners.

As part of the study, the CDC researchers provided free tests for HIV/AIDS to the men who participated. The study revealed that 22 percent of the participants tested positive for HIV/AIDS.

Experts have cited the use of drugs and alcohol during sex as a reason many gay men are engaging in unprotected sex. They point out that when partners are under the influence of drugs or alcohol, the search for condoms may be the furthest thing from their minds. Said Russell, a twenty-six-year-old gay man, "I was into a lot of drinking and drugs and I was just really being very unsafe in general."

Quoted in Benjamin J. Klassen et al., "Condoms Are like Public Transit: It's Something You Want Everyone Else to Take," *BMC Public Health*, January 28, 2019. https://bmcpublichealth.biomedcentral.com.

that result in severe injuries or death. Those were the findings of statistics reported by the Trevor Project, a West Hollywood, California–based group that works to prevent suicides among LGBTQ teens. According to statistics compiled in 2020 by the Trevor Project, suicide attempts by young people in the LGBTQ community are four to six times more likely to result in injury, poisoning, or overdose that requires treatment from a doctor or nurse, compared to others who self-harm. This means that young members of the LGBTQ community try more severe methods of harming themselves, such as using firearms, taking massive overdoses of drugs, or resorting to self-strangulation by hanging themselves. The Trevor Project also points out that 40 percent of transgender adults reported having made a suicide attempt, and 92 percent of those individuals reported having attempted suicide before age twenty-five.

A gay man named Jayvyn says he often contemplated suicide while growing up in a group home, where he endured years of physical and verbal abuse from the other parentless youths in the home. Says Jayvyn, "For the first two, three, four years, I never fought back. I would just take it. They would hit me. . . . I would be the pit of all the jokes. I would just feel so low. There were points I was sitting there, I was just thinking, 'I want to die.'"[43]

Jayvyn was able to overcome his feelings of depression, but other members of the LGBTQ community give in to their mental anguish and take their own lives. The case of Andrew Leach of Southaven, Mississippi, serves as a particularly sad example. Leach, who believed himself to be bisexual, was just twelve years old in 2018 when he committed suicide by hanging himself in his family's garage. Leach had been the victim of intense bullying by classmates. "He finally came out with the information at school that he thought he may be bisexual," says his father, Matt Leach. "I think that really amped up the bullying. . . . Kids were telling him, 'We're going to put hands on you. You're not going to make it out of this bathroom.' Things of that nature."[44]

> "They would hit me. . . . I would be the pit of all the jokes. I would just feel so low. There were points I was sitting there, I was just thinking, 'I want to die.'"[43]
>
> —Jayvyn, gay man who grew up in a group home

Surviving Suicide

For members of the LGBTQ community who attempt suicide and survive, the road back to feeling strong and secure can be a long one. For starters, unsuccessful attempts at suicide often result in physical trauma, such as broken bones or other injuries, that could take months to heal. But living with the aftermath of a suicide attempt often ramps up the mental trauma that led to the LGBTQ person's initial attempt at suicide. Mary Emily O'Hara, a journalist from New York City, realized that she was a lesbian as a teenager. She made the first of two attempts at suicide when she was fourteen. She made her second unsuccessful attempt to end her own life seven years later. "At age 21, I tried again—and really went for it," she says. "The details are ugly, but suffice it to say it involved medical treatment in a hospital, followed by a mandatory stay in a mental ward. The dehumanizing experience of being in a mental hospital, more than any other factor, was enough to scare me away from ever attempting suicide again."[45]

O'Hara says she was a teenager during the 1990s, a decade in which many members of the LGBTQ community felt endangered because of their sexual preference or gender identity. It was the decade in which Matthew Shepard was murdered. It was also the decade in which comedian Ellen DeGeneres acknowledged publicly that she is a lesbian. A situation comedy starring DeGeneres was canceled by its network after advertisers withdrew their com-

In the 1990s, comedian Ellen DeGeneres acknowledged publicly that she is a lesbian. Her situation comedy was soon canceled after advertisers withdrew their commercial support from the show.

mercial support from the show; DeGeneres also received death threats. Says O'Hara, "This was the atmosphere in which I grew up: admitting that you were gay or lesbian was still a terrifying—often life-threatening risk."[46]

After recovering from her physical wounds and overcoming her depression, O'Hara resolved to live her life as a proud member of the LGBTQ community. She says, "I think the takeaway from my own story is this: life is . . . hard sometimes, but it is so worth living. Looking back, my only regret is that I ever tried to hurt myself and the people who cared about me. But I don't regret continuing to live. Not for a second."[47]

> "The dehumanizing experience of being in a mental hospital, more than any other factor, was enough to scare me away from ever attempting suicide again."[45]
>
> —Mary Emily O'Hara, lesbian who twice attempted to commit suicide

Sharing Needles

As O'Hara's case illustrates, depression, anxiety, and self-harm are some of the ills suffered by members of the LGBTQ community who are victims of abuse. But there are many other ways in which LGBTQ people harm themselves in the wake of abuse. For example, the CDC reports that members of the LGBTQ community who have been abused are very likely to seek solace by using illegal drugs. They are also very likely to ignore health concerns about having casual and unprotected sex with strangers, many of whom they find through dating apps.

These two practices could be extremely dangerous. By using illegal drugs, people risk death through overdosing or contracting highly communicable diseases such as hepatitis by sharing needles. Hepatitis is a virus that causes inflammation of the liver, a condition that could lead to death.

Moreover, by engaging in casual and unprotected sex with strangers, LGBTQ people expose themselves to sexually transmitted diseases. This includes syphilis, which manifests itself in numerous sores forming across the surface of the body, and gonorrhea, whose symptoms include a burning sensation during urination. Hepatitis can also be sexually transmitted. Those diseases and

49

The Dangers of Chemsex

Many gay men who have been physically or mentally abused are turning to a trend known as "chemsex" to deal with their anguish. Chemsex is the desire to meet up with strangers for casual sex while under the influence of illegal drugs, usually methamphetamine or gamma-hydroxybutyrate, also known as GHB. Many gay men use the abbreviation *PNP*, which stands for "party and play," while searching for like-minded individuals on gay dating apps.

Craig Sloan, a New York City psychotherapist, says gay men turn to chemsex to relieve their anxieties, often after they have been victims of abuse. He says, "I've often had clients tell me that when they experienced sex on meth, GHB or both for the first time that all the negative voices in their heads about shame, not being good enough, not fitting in and other traumas disappeared, albeit temporarily."

Methamphetamine and GHB are both highly addictive drugs. After engaging in chemsex for years, Nick Dothée, a gay man from Los Angeles, nearly lost his life after a drug overdose in 2017. Following his overdose he entered a drug rehabilitation program and has managed to remain drug-free since then. Says Dothée, "I was one of those gay men arranging to PNP, lost and sometimes barely conscious for days at a time, unsure where I was—and not really caring—as long as I was high."

Quoted in Nick Dothée, "Gay 'Chemsex' Culture in Hollywood Almost Killed Me. This Is How I Survived," NBC News, February 29, 2020. www.nbcnews.com.

Dothée, "Gay 'Chemsex' Culture in Hollywood Almost Killed Me. This Is How I Survived."

others can lead to complications that can be far more serious. If left untreated, many sexually transmitted diseases can result in death.

Clearly, though, the most feared of the sexually transmitted diseases is the human immunodeficiency virus (HIV), which causes a condition known as acquired immune deficiency syndrome (AIDS). Moreover, HIV/AIDS can also be transmitted through sharing needles. Since the disease first emerged in the 1980s, some 32 million people worldwide have died of HIV/AIDS. Deaths are less common today than they were in the 1980s and 1990s, thanks to the development of drugs that have been able to effectively treat the disease. However, HIV/AIDS remains a very real threat to people in the LGBTQ community as well as others. According to the CDC, the mortality rate for HIV/AIDS patients in the United States peaked in 1995 at about fifty thousand; in 2017 HIV/AIDS caused the deaths of about sixteen thousand people in America.

The Danger of HIV/AIDS

By engaging in casual and unprotected sex, members of the LGBTQ community—and in particular, gay men—are highly susceptible to the disease. According to the CDC, there were 37,832 new cases of HIV/AIDS reported in 2018; 69 percent of those were LGBTQ individuals. Says the Human Rights Campaign, "Gay and bisexual men made up an estimated 2 percent of the US population [in the 2010 decade] . . . but 55 percent of all people living with HIV in the United States. If current diagnosis rates continue, one in six gay and bisexual men will be diagnosed with HIV in their lifetime."[48]

Adrian Hyyrylainen-Trett understands this danger better than most. As a gay teen he was bullied and physically abused while a student in the British town of Cringleford. Recalling an incident in which he was bullied by another student at school, Hyyrylainen-Trett says, "He slammed a toilet door in my face. I blacked out. I came round on the floor of the toilet, got up, and walked to my next lesson, pretending nothing had happened. I didn't want anyone to know why it had happened."[49]

Returning home from school each day, Hyyrylainen-Trett says he often contemplated suicide. Several times, Hyyrylainen-Trett says, his parents found him standing by an open window on the second floor of his family's home. Each time, Hyyrylainen-Trett says, he was close to jumping out the window—but never told his parents of his suicidal thoughts. He says:

I knew my parents and the people around me wouldn't understand. I knew I couldn't tell anyone. There was nowhere I could go; nowhere I could talk. I became depressed and anxious. With psychological bullying all you have is the words whirling around your head—comments thrown at you in the sports room, in the gym, walking home from school. My parents always picked me up and kids would shout jokes as I was walking down towards them.[50]

Building a Productive Life

Hyyrylainen-Trett's anxieties also led him to seek companionship with other gay men. As an adult he moved to London and often engaged in casual and unprotected sex. He says, "I was hop-

By engaging in casual and unprotected sex, gay men are at greatest risk of contracting HIV. The group makes up only 2 percent of the general population but represents 55 percent of all HIV infections.

ing to please [someone] enough so he'd want to be my boyfriend. I was going from one person to another trying to find someone to love me. Sometimes I'd find older people who I thought might look after me, or protect me, knowing that mentally I could quite easily go down the drain. I ended up doing all this because I was so lonely and my self-esteem was so low."[51] He also fell into heavy drug use—overdosing five times over a period of a few years.

Finally, his lifestyle of heavy drug use and unprotected sex resulted in a diagnosis of HIV/AIDS. His affliction with HIV/AIDS, he says, is "a consequence of all these things—bullying, mental ill-health, low self-esteem. All those things could have been prevented. Yet all these things are still happening and no one is talking about it. I feel I owe it to the community to talk about it."[52] Hyyrylainen-Trett eventually did turn his life around. His disease has been controlled, thanks to the medications he takes. Meanwhile, he became a staunch advocate for the LGBTQ community in Great Britain and has run for public office as a candidate for a seat in the British Parliament.

Hyyrylainen-Trett and O'Hara represent members of the LGBTQ community who managed to overcome their mental anguish and build productive lives: O'Hara after two suicide attempts; Hyyrylainen-Trett after contracting HIV/AIDS. But others, among them twelve-year-old Andrew Leach, were robbed of the chance to build lives for themselves due to the constant bullying as well as physical and verbal abuse they were forced to endure. Physical and verbal abuse are common elements in the lives of many members of the LGBTQ community. Sadly, to deal with the mental anguish caused by this abuse, LGBTQ people often respond to their distress by turning to drugs, casual and unprotected sex, and attempts to take their own lives.

> "Sometimes I'd find older people who I thought might look after me, or protect me, knowing that mentally I could quite easily go down the drain. I ended up doing all this because I was so lonely and my self-esteem was so low."[51]
>
> —Adrian Hyyrylainen-Trett, bullied gay man who contracted HIV/AIDS

Chapter Five

Confronting Violence

In a kindergarten class at Ashlawn Elementary School in Arlington, Virginia, the young students sat cross-legged on the floor around Sarah McBride, a volunteer for the Human Rights Campaign, as she read from a storybook titled *I Am Jazz*. "I have a girl brain but a boy body. This is called transgender," McBride read to the students. "I was born this way."[53] The drawings in the book show Jazz wearing skirts and blouses, sporting a girl's ponytail and hairband, swimming in a pool while wearing a mermaid costume, and playing soccer. The book's illustrations also show a wide range of acceptance from Jazz's friends as well as the transgender girl's parents. "My best friends are Samantha and Casey," the book says. "We like high heels and princess gowns, or cartwheels and trampolines. But I'm not exactly like Samantha and Casey."[54] The book was authored by Jessica Herthel and Jazz Jennings, a transgender teen from Florida.

The class that featured McBride reading to the students about a transgender girl their age shows how far some school administrators have come in recent years in finding ways to educate young people about the history and culture of the LGBTQ community. Virginia school districts have been leaders in

> "LGBT history is part of American history. To tell our students anything other than that would be fictional."[55]
>
> —Jon Oliveira, spokesperson for Garden State Equality

incorporating education about the LGBTQ community into their curricula. Other states, such as New Jersey, have become active in the effort. Says Jon Oliveira, a spokesperson for Garden State Equality, an LGBTQ advocacy group in New Jersey, "LGBT history is part of American history. To tell our students anything other than that would be fictional. There is so much information to be consumed in the classroom."[55]

Learning About the Pink Triangle

New Jersey is one of four states that have mandated that schools include education about LGBTQ history and culture in their classrooms. The other states mandating such programs are California, Colorado, and Illinois. In history class at Haddon Heights High School in New Jersey, for example, fifteen-year-old student Olivia Loesch learned about the pink triangle—the fabric badge that Nazi leaders forced gay inmates to wear on

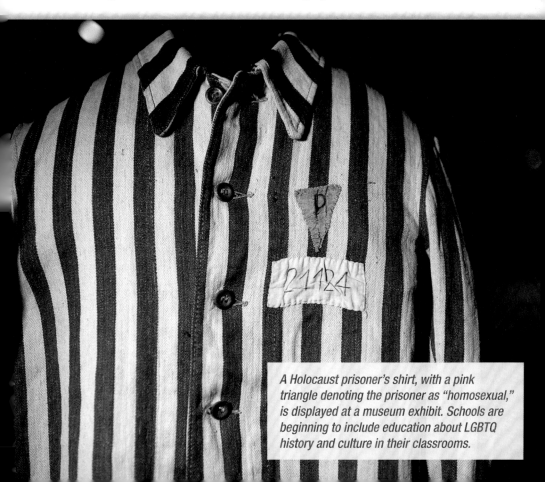

A Holocaust prisoner's shirt, with a pink triangle denoting the prisoner as "homosexual," is displayed at a museum exhibit. Schools are beginning to include education about LGBTQ history and culture in their classrooms.

their uniforms in the World War II concentration camps. "I never knew about it," says Loesch, who identifies as genderqueer, meaning she does not identify specifically as either male or female. "I feel that topic should be talked about and people should talk about me."[56]

Some school districts are not waiting for their state legislatures to mandate instruction on LGBTQ history and culture but are acting on their own. To help these school districts structure programs providing LGBTQ education, GLSEN has written a model curriculum that schools can adopt to help teachers and administrators develop course work and policies when it comes to teaching about the LGBTQ community. The model curriculum covers issues ranging from how transgender students may dress for school to whether restrooms should be gender neutral to how to address cases of bullying and harassment. On the topic of bullying, here is what the GLSEN model curriculum advises:

Discrimination, bullying, and harassment on the basis of gender identity or expression is prohibited within the District. It is the responsibility of each school and all staff to ensure that all students, including transgender and gender nonconforming students, have safe school environments. The scope of this responsibility includes ensuring that any incident of discrimination, harassment, or bullying is given immediate attention, including investigating the incident, taking age- and developmentally-appropriate action, and providing students and staff with appropriate resources and supports. Enforcement of anti-bullying policies should focus on education and prevention rather than exclusionary discipline. Complaints alleging discrimination or harassment based on a student's actual or perceived gender identity or expression are to be taken seriously and handled in the same manner as other discrimination, bullying, or harassment complaints.[57]

Do Transgender Athletes Enjoy Advantages?

Opponents of permitting transgender athletes to compete in sports argue that transgender girls would be naturally stronger and faster than other female athletes. Similarly, they argue transgender boys would be at a disadvantage against male athletes. But Georgetown University law professor M. Gregg Bloche, who is also a physician, says such arguments are not necessarily based on science.

For starters, Bloche says, substantial musculoskeletal differences between the genders do not emerge until puberty is well under way. Therefore, many younger students would find neither advantages nor disadvantages when competing against transgender classmates.

But even after athletes reach puberty, he says, differences in athletic abilities may not be so dramatic. He argues that athletic skills are often the product of much more than physical size and speed. "Myriad influences—environmental, genetic, and mixtures of both—produce differences in athletic capability and performance," he says. "Without these differences, sports would be insufferably dull. Every competition would yield a tie—or, worse, a winner decided by dumb luck."

Moreover, he says, many sports are specifically keyed to the physical dimensions of the athletes. He points out that wrestling opponents are paired according to their weights. Therefore, he sees little reason a transgender boy could not compete against a male athlete in a wrestling match. He says, "We should recognize that in sports, as in the rest of life, we all have competitive edges and weaknesses—and that judgments about which are and aren't fair are matters of culture and politics, not biology."

M. Gregg Bloche, "Do Transgender Athletes Have an Unfair Advantage?," *The Hill* (Washington, DC), January 20, 2020. https://thehill.com.

The Plight of Transgender Athletes

There has been some pushback from opponents of incorporating LGBTQ culture and history into school curricula. The Family Policy Alliance—an organization composed of conservative Christian leaders—has opposed these efforts. It gathered more than seven thousand names on petitions demanding that the New Jersey state legislature repeal the law requiring LGBTQ education in public schools. Says a statement from the group, "In many ways, this instruction will directly challenge biblical teaching on homosexuality and what parents choose to teach children at home."[58]

And in Idaho, state lawmakers adopted legislation that prohibits boy athletes who identify as girls from participating in school sports as members of girls' teams. Girls who identify as boys are similarly barred from joining boys' teams. "We are not trying to do anything except save women's sports for girls and women," says state senator Mary Souza.

There is controversy over allowing transgender students to participate on school sports teams. Opponents argue that male and female athletes would be uncomfortable sharing locker rooms with transgender athletes.

"It is in the state's interest."[59] By early 2020 Idaho governor Brad Little had yet to sign the legislation into law.

Two of the biggest concerns involve the sharing of locker rooms and unfair advantages on the field. Supporters of the proposed law argue that male athletes would feel uncomfortable sharing locker rooms with transgender boys and that female athletes would feel uncomfortable sharing locker rooms with transgender girls. In competition, the concern revolves around physiology. A transgender girl (who was born male) could potentially be faster and stronger than the other girls on the field and therefore have an unfair advantage. This has been a concern for Cheryl Radachowsky, whose daughter Alanna Smith competes in track and field events for her Connecticut high school team. In 2017 Connecticut schools started permitting student athletes to compete in events in the gender in which they identify. This has put her daughter at a disadvantage, says Radachowsky. She explains:

> As a parent, it is gut-wrenching to know that no matter how hard my daughter works to achieve her goals, she will lose athletic opportunities to a [harmful] gender idcology. Left unchecked, this ideology will in the long run eliminate fair play for all biological females in all sports. As we are seeing in Connecticut, a biological boy's subjective sense of his gender doesn't cancel out his physical advantage over girls.[60]

Hate Crimes Continue to Rise

Despite these objections, many schools are pushing ahead with plans to incorporate education about the LGBTQ community into their curricula. Clearly, the thinking of many school administrators is that members of the LGBTQ community will experience a decrease in bullying, violent attacks, and other abuse if people are better educated about what it means to be gay, lesbian, or transgender.

Twenty States Do Not Protect the LGBTQ Community

By 2020 twenty states had not adopted laws that qualify offenses directed at members of the LGBTQ community as hate crimes. Moreover, legislators in five states—Arkansas, Georgia, Indiana, South Carolina, and Wyoming—have declined to pass their own comprehensive hate crime laws. This means that offenses based on biases against faith, race, and ethnicity committed in those states are not qualified as hate crimes.

Some political leaders in those five states have specifically said they oppose enacting hate crime laws because they would be forced to include LGBTQ people, whom they do not believe should be protected by hate crimes laws. "Why is the Indiana General Assembly again debating so-called 'hate-crimes' legislation?" says Indiana Family Institute president Curt Smith, an opponent of hate crimes legislation in his state. "The short answer is the LGBTQ community seeks to politicize the criminal code to elevate its legal status." (A hate crimes bill failed to win adoption in the Indiana legislature in 2018.)

LGBTQ activist Lesléa Newman disputes these arguments. "Frankly, I don't understand why every state in the country and every country in the world doesn't have hate-crime laws. I have heard the arguments—mostly backed up by quotes from the Bible taken out of context—that the LGBTQ community doesn't deserve to be protected or even to exist."

The other states that do not protect the LGBTQ community under their hate crime statutes include Alabama, Alaska, Idaho, Michigan, Mississippi, Montana, North Carolina, North Dakota, Ohio, Oklahoma, Pennsylvania, South Dakota, Utah, Virginia, and West Virginia.

Quoted in Tony Cook, "Indiana Lawmakers Take Up Hate Crimes Bill in Aftermath of Charlottesville," *Indianapolis Star*, January 22, 2018. www.indystar.com.

Quoted in Christina Maxouris and Brandon Griggs, "Two Decades After Matthew Shepard's Death, 20 States Still Don't Consider Attacks on LGBTQ People as Hate Crimes," CNN, October 12, 2018. www.cnn.com.

Many school administrators hope this strategy works, because despite the harsh penalties imposed on defendants by the federal Shepard-Byrd Act as well as the many state anti-hate crimes laws, statistics show that the LGBTQ community continues to be confronted with violence. After adoption of the Shepard-Byrd Act, the

FBI recorded 11,633 hate crimes committed in the United States against members of the LGBTQ community from 2009 to 2018. Therefore, during that ten-year period, an average of about 1,200 hate crimes are committed each year against LGBTQ people. Although Congress passed a tough law against the commission of hate crimes targeting members of the LGBTQ community, gay and transgender people still find themselves victimized by hate.

Calls for Tougher Laws

Given the high numbers of hate crime offenses that are still committed in America, many advocates are calling for even tougher laws. Says San Diego, California, attorney Samuel Duimovich, who published a study on the effectiveness of the Shepard-Byrd Act:

> In the years since the [Shepard-Byrd Act] was enacted, the number of crimes motivated by bias against a person's sexual orientation remained fairly constant with over a thousand incidents of reported violence per year, with the highest percentage of incidents affecting gay men. . . . These statistics . . . show the animosity that gays and lesbians face. At least in its immediate aftermath, the inclusion of sexual orientation as a protected class under the [Shepard-Byrd] did not seem to affect the number of hate crimes against gays and lesbians.[61]

According to Duimovich, the Shepard-Byrd Act provides prosecutors with too much discretion to decide whether offenses against members of the LGBTQ community, as well as others, qualify as hate crimes. In other words, if an assailant physically assaults a gay individual, the prosecutor must decide whether the assault was motivated by the assailant's homophobia. If the prosecutor decides that homophobia was the motivation, the defendant could be sentenced to a lengthy prison term. However, if the prosecutor does not feel that bias against gay people was the motivation, the perpetrator could receive a much lighter sentence—perhaps probation, which does not require the defendant to serve jail time at all. Moreover, Duimovich argues, the victims have no recourse other than to accept the prosecutor's decision. To remedy this failing, Duimovich recommends that judges, rather than prosecutors, be given the final decision on whether the case should be pursued as a hate crime.

Paris Cyrus was the victim of such an assault. The transgender woman from Columbus, Ohio, called police after she was allegedly assaulted by her mother and her mother's boyfriend in 2020. She says:

I was trying to stop from being strangled. I was being strangled and kicked in the face at the same time. They were saying you are not a woman. You're not a woman. You are a guy with mascara on. . . . My mom I feel has always been homophobic, and when I was about 9 years old I would hear her tell her friends, there is something wrong with him, that is how it started, there is something wrong with him. . . .

We all three fell down the stairs and as I am trying to get up, he has a chokehold. His whole elbow and everything was around my neck as I am getting stomped in my face. There was blood all over the couch, in the kitchen in the bathroom.[62]

After their arrests, Cyrus's mother and her boyfriend were not charged with committing a hate crime. Instead, prosecutors elected to charge the two defendants merely with assault.

Jurors May Be Biased

In addition to giving prosecutors less discretion in deciding whether a crime is motivated by bias, Duimovich also suggests prosecutors need to do a better job of ensuring that members of juries are not biased against members of the LGBTQ community. Very often, he says, jurors who harbor prejudices against gay and transgender victims are selected for juries that return acquittals against defendants charged with hate crimes. He cited the example of Kevin Pennington, who was kidnapped and beaten by two of his cousins in 2011 in rural Kentucky. According to Pennington, the alleged perpetrators shouted gay slurs during the assault. "This case is about the two defendants . . . planning and trying to kill Kevin Pennington because Kevin Pennington is gay,"[63] Assistant US Attorney Hydee Hawkins told jurors. Eventually, the jury convicted the cousins of kidnapping but acquitted them of the hate crime charges. Ultimately, one attacker was sentenced to seventeen years in prison; the other received a prison term of

JURORS

Legal experts believe prosecutors need to do a better job of ensuring that members of juries are not biased against members of the LGBTQ community.

thirty years. Had they been convicted of the hate crimes charges, their sentences would have likely been longer.

Duimovich argues that during the trial, defense attorneys made it clear they were appealing to the prejudices that jurors harbored against members of the LGBTQ community. Prosecutors, he says, should have done a better job of weeding out potential jurors who harbored biases against the gay community. This process could have occurred during pretrial questioning of citizens summoned for jury duty on the day of the trial. Says Duimovich, "The [Shepard-Byrd Act's] effectiveness is stymied by prosecutorial inaction, a high criminal burden of proof, and potential jury bias."[64]

While advocates like Duimovich argue that it is time for lawmakers to revise the federal and state hate crime laws, it is clear that many school administrators believe they can make a difference in their classrooms. That is why kindergarten students who are learning about a transgender student named Jazz may, in the years ahead, find themselves willing to accept members of the LGBTQ community as equals.

"The [Shepard-Byrd Act's] effectiveness is stymied by prosecutorial inaction, a high criminal burden of proof, and potential jury bias."[64]

—Samuel Duimovich, attorney

Introduction: The Very Real Dangers Facing the LGBTQ Community

1. R.J. Parker, *Killing the Rainbow: A History of the Homophile Movement*. Toronto, Canada: RJ Parker, 2016, p. 7.
2. Quoted in Muri Assunção, "Anti-LGBTQ Violence in US Is Rising, According to FBI's Hate Crime Report," *New York Daily News*, November 3, 2019. www.nydailynews.com.
3. Quoted in Dana Branham, "Trial Begins This Week for Man Accused of Beating Muhlaysia Booker in Attack Caught on Viral Video," *Dallas (TX) Morning News*, October 13, 2019. www.dallasnews.com.

Chapter One: A History of Violence Against the LGBTQ Community

4. Marilyn B. Skinner, *Sexuality in Greek and Roman Culture*. West Sussex, England: Wiley, 2014. Kindle edition.
5. Quoted in Jack Nichols, "George Weinberg, PhD," Gay Today, February 3, 1997. http://gaytoday.badpuppy.com.
6. George Weinberg, *Society and the Healthy Homosexual*. New York: St. Martin's, 1972, p. 5.
7. Quoted in Anna North, "Queer True Crime Stories of the Past Show How the Press Stoked Fear of Gay Men," Vox, June 11, 2019. www.vox.com.
8. Quoted in Joe Sommerlad, "Pride 2019: What Happened at the Stonewall Riots and How Did They Inspire the LGBT+ Rights Movement?," *The Independent* (London), 2019. www.independent.co.uk.
9. Quoted in Les Ledbetter, "Bill on Homosexual Rights Advances in San Francisco," *New York Times*, March 22, 1978, p. A-21.
10. Quoted in Daniel J. Flynn, "Mythology as History," *City Journal*, November 26, 2018. www.city-journal.org.

11. Quoted in Kimberly O'Brien, "Police: Backstreet Cafe Gunman Hunted Gays," *Roanoke (VA) Times*, September 24, 2000. www.roanoke.com.
12. Weinberg, *Society and the Healthy Homosexual*, p. 11.
13. Quoted in Doug Meyer, *Violence Against Queer People*. New Brunswick, NJ: Rutgers University Press, 2015, p. 1.
14. Meyer, *Violence Against Queer People*, p. 2.

Chapter Two: Internet Threats

15. Quoted in Alex Bollinger, "Bullied Gay Teen Punches His Tormentor Who Called Him a 'Fa***t,'" LGBTQ Nation, November 11, 2019. www.lgbtqnation.com.
16. Quoted in Bollinger, "Bullied Gay Teen Punches His Tormentor Who Called Him a 'Fa***t.'"
17. Quoted in Gwen Aviles, "Viral Video of Teen Punching Classmate Draws Attention to Anti-Gay Bullying," NBC News, November 14, 2019. www.nbcnews.com.
18. Quoted in Futurity, "Gay Youth Reluctant to Report Cyberbullying," 2020. www.futurity.org.
19. Quoted in Fox 61 News, "High School Football Players Suspended for Pride Flag Burning, 'All Gays Die' Snapchat Video," June 19, 2019. www.fox61.com.
20. Quoted in Nate Schweber and Lisa W. Foderaro, "Roommate in Tyler Clementi Case Pleads Guilty to Attempted Invasion of Privacy," *New York Times*, October 27, 2016, p. A25.
21. Quoted in *New York Times* Editorial Staff, *Cyberbullying: A Deadly Trend*. New York: Rosen, 2019, pp. 10–11.
22. Quoted in Tim Fitzsimons et al., "Tennessee Teen Dies by Suicide After Being Outed Online," NBC News, September 30, 2019. www.nbcnews.com.
23. Quoted in Jamie Ducharme, "A 9-Year-Old Colorado Boy's Death by Suicide Highlights the Challenges Facing LGBTQ Kids," *Time*, August 28, 2018. https://time.com.
24. Quoted in Ducharme, "A 9-Year-Old Colorado Boy's Death by Suicide Highlights the Challenges Facing LGBTQ Kids."
25. Quoted in Netsanity, "Cyberbullying: LGBT Youth," 2019. https://netsanity.net.

26. Quoted in Crystal Bonvillian, "Men Who Used Grindr App to Target, Assault Victims Sentenced," *Dayton (OH) Daily News*, May 4, 2018. www.daytondailynews.com.

27. Quoted in Gwen Aviles, "Gay Man Killed, Another Critically Injured in Grindr Meetup," NBC News, July 16, 2019. www .nbcnews.com.

28. Ari Ezra Waldman, "Queer Dating Apps Are Unsafe by Design," *New York Times*, June 20, 2019. www.nytimes.com.

Chapter Three: Targeted by Hate

29. Quoted in Lynnette Curtis, "Gay Center Finds Home in Downtown Las Vegas," *Las Vegas (NV) Review-Journal*, February 24, 2013. www.reviewjournal.com.

30. Quoted in John Riley, "LGBTQ Center of Southern Nevada Vandalized with Anti-gay Graffiti," *Metro Weekly*, September 6, 2019. www.metroweekly.com.

31. Quoted in Riley, "LGBTQ Center of Southern Nevada Vandalized with Anti-Gay Graffiti."

32. Eric David Rosenberg, "Hate Crimes, Hate Speech and Free Speech," *Nova Law Review*, 1992, p. 629. https://nsuworks .nova.edu.

33. Quoted in Patrick Kelleher, "Malaysian Rock Band's Defence of Song Encouraging the Death of Gay People Is the Most Pathetic Thing We've Seen This Week," PinkNews, March 10, 2020. www.pinknews.co.uk.

34. Christopher Heath Wellman, "A Defense of Stiffer Penalties for Hate Crimes," *Hypatia*, Spring 2006, p. 68.

35. Quoted in Jeff Zeleny, "Obama Signs Hate Crimes Bill," *The Caucus* (blog), *New York Times*, October 28, 2009. https:// thecaucus.blogs.nytimes.com.

36. Quoted in Kaelan Deese, "Man Arrested After Allegedly Harassing Transgender Journalist at New York Subway Station," *The Hill* (Washington, DC), February 1, 2020. https://thehill .com.

37. Quoted in BBC News, "London Bus Attack: Boys Told Couple to 'Show How Lesbians Have Sex,'" November 29, 2019. www.bbc.com.

38. Quoted in Jayati Ramakrishnan, "Missing Vancouver Teen Was Strangled to Death After Suspect Found Out She Was Transgender, Police Say," *The Oregonian* (Portland, OR), December 18, 2019. www.oregonlive.com.

Chapter Four: Pain and Anguish: The Effects of Violence

39. Quoted in NBC 5 Chicago, "Barrington Family's Lawn Vandalized in 'Hate Crime,'" June 1, 2019. www.nbcchicago.com.

40. Quoted in NBC 5 Chicago, "Barrington Family's Lawn Vandalized in 'Hate Crime.'"

41. Jonathan Charlesworth, *That's So Gay! Challenging Homophobic Bullying*. London: Kingsley, 2015, pp. 72–73.

42. Brian S. Mustanski et al., "Mental Health Disorders, Psychological Distress, and Suicidality in a Diverse Sample of Lesbian, Gay, Bisexual, and Transgender Youths," *American Journal of Public Health*, December 2010, p. 2430.

43. Quoted in Meyer, *Violence Against Queer People*, pp. 10–11.

44. Quoted in Curtis M. Wong, "Parents of 12-Year-Old Say Son Killed Himself After Being Bullied over Sexuality," HuffPost, March 14, 2018. www.huffpost.com.

45. Mary Emily O'Hara, "How I Learned to Love Life After Surviving Suicide," Them, June 8, 2018. www.them.us.

46. O'Hara, "How I Learned to Love Life After Surviving Suicide."

47. O'Hara, "How I Learned to Love Life After Surviving Suicide."

48. Human Rights Campaign, "How HIV Impacts LGBTQ People," 2017. www.hrc.org.

49. Quoted in Patrick Strudwick, "Meet Britain's First HIV-Positive Parliamentary Candidate," BuzzFeed News, March 30, 2015. www.buzzfeednews.com.

50. Quoted in Strudwick, "Meet Britain's First HIV-Positive Parliamentary Candidate."

51. Quoted in Strudwick, "Meet Britain's First HIV-Positive Parliamentary Candidate."

52. Quoted in Strudwick, "Meet Britain's First HIV-Positive Parliamentary Candidate."

Chapter Five: Confronting Violence

53. Quoted in Debbie Truong, "In a Virginia School, a Celebration of Transgender Students in a Kindergarten Class," *Washington Post*, March 3, 2019. www.washingtonpost.com.

54. Jessica Herthel and Jazz Jennings, *I Am Jazz*. New York: Dial, 2014. Kindle edition.

55. Quoted in Melanie Burney, "LGBTQ on the Syllabus: South Jersey District in a Pilot Program for the Lessons," *Philadelphia Inquirer*, January 20, 2020, p. A10.

56. Quoted in Burney, "LGBTQ on the Syllabus," p. A1.

57. GLSEN, *Model School District Policy on Transgender and Gender Nonconforming Students*. GLSEN: Washington, DC, 2018, pp. 3–4.

58. Quoted in Burney, "LGBTQ on the Syllabus," p. A10.

59. Quoted in John Riley, "Idaho Lawmakers Ban Transgender Athletes from Competing in Women's Sports," *Metro Weekly*, March 17, 2020. www.metroweekly.com.

60. Cheryl Radachowsky, "'Justice' for Trans Athletes Is Unfair to Girls like My Daughter," *New York Post*, October 13, 2019. https://nypost.com.

61. Samuel Duimovich, "A Critique of the Hate Crimes Prevention Act Regarding Its Protection of Gays and Lesbians (and How a Private Right Could Fix It)," *Review of Law and Justice*, Winter 2014, pp. 303–4.

62. Quoted in Lu Ann Stoia, "Transgender Woman Says Hate Crime Laws in Ohio Need to Change," Fox 28 News, January 8, 2020. https://myfox28columbus.com.

63. Quoted in Bill Estep, "Hate Crime Trial: Victim Tells of Beating, Anti-gay Slurs," *Lexington (KY) Herald-Leader*, October 17, 2012. www.kentucky.com.

64. Duimovich, "A Critique of the Hate Crimes Prevention Act Regarding Its Protection of Gays and Lesbians (and How a Private Right Could Fix It)," p. 312.

Organizations and Websites

The Advocate—www.advocate.com

Established in the 1960s, *The Advocate* was the first national magazine to cover the LGBTQ community. By accessing the "Commentary" tab on the publication's website, visitors can find many essays on issues facing LGBTQ people, including how political leaders and schools react to the issue of violence against gay and transgender people.

GLSEN—www.glsen.org

GLSEN advocates for schools to adopt curricula that teach about LGBTQ history and culture. By accessing the "Our Work" tab on the GLSEN website, students can find numerous studies into the effects of violence on LGBTQ young people, including the group's annual School Climate Survey, which addresses whether LGBTQ people feel safe and accepted in their schools.

Hate Crimes FBI—www.fbi.gov/investigate/civil-rights/hate-crimes

The federal government's chief law enforcement agency maintains this website to provide statistics on hate crimes. The statistics cover the years 2011 through 2018 and include data on the nature of the crimes, places they occurred, victims, and offenders.

Human Rights Campaign—www.hrc.org

The organization campaigns for LGBTQ equality. By accessing the "Hate Crimes" tab on the group's website, students can find information on which states qualify crimes against the LGBTQ community as crimes of bias. The site includes state-by-state maps explaining each state's hate crimes law.

Lesbian, Gay, Bisexual, and Transgender Health Centers for Disease Control and Prevention—www.cdc.gov/lgbthealth

The CDC maintains this website to address health issues faced by members of the LGBTQ community. By accessing the tab for "LGBT Youth," visitors can find statistics and reports on students who face cyberbullying and other threats, how bullying and violence affects mental health, and strategies that schools and parents can take to help LGBTQ teens.

Matthew Shepard Foundation—www.matthewshepard.org

Established in the wake of the murder of gay student Matthew Shepard, the organization provides resources for young members of the LGBTQ community, such as advice on how to respond to bullying, what steps to take if they are feeling suicidal, and lists of resources to aid LGBTQ students at American universities.

PFLAG—https://pflag.org

The organization works to help families accept their sons and daughters who are members of the LGBTQ community. By accessing the "Our Work" tab on the group's website, students can learn about the group's Safe Schools Campaign, in which local PFLAG chapters work with schools to make campuses safe for LGBTQ students.

Trevor Project—www.thetrevorproject.org

Established by the producers of the 1994 Academy Award–winning film *Trevor*, which told the story of a bullied gay student, the Trevor Project provides a hotline for members of the LGBTQ community who are suffering from depression. The website also provides online resources, such as videos and model curricula, for schools that wish to adopt LGBTQ lesson plans.

Books

Heidi C. Feldman, *LGBT Discrimination*. San Diego, CA: ReferencePoint, 2018.

Hal Marcovitz, *Hate Crimes*. San Diego, CA: ReferencePoint, 2019.

New York Times Editorial Staff, *Cyberbullying: A Deadly Trend*. New York: Rosen, 2019.

Helis Sikk and Leisa Meyer, eds., *The Legacies of Matthew Shepard: Twenty Years Later*. New York: Routledge, 2019.

Dashka Slater, *The 57 Bus: A True Story of Two Teenagers and the Crime That Changed Their Lives*. New York: Farrar, Straus and Giroux, 2017.

Marc Stein, *The Stonewall Riots: A Documentary History*. New York: New York University Press, 2019.

Internet Sources

Gwen Aviles, "Viral Video of Teen Punching Classmate Draws Attention to Anti-gay Bullying," NBC News, November 14, 2019. www.nbcnews.com.

Anna North, "Queer True Crime Stories of the Past Show How the Press Stoked Fear of Gay Men," Vox, June 11, 2019. www.vox.com.

Mary Emily O'Hara, "How I Learned to Love Life After Surviving Suicide," Them, June 8, 2018. www.them.us.

Cheryl Radachowsky, "'Justice' for Trans Athletes Is Unfair to Girls like My Daughter," *New York Post*, October 13, 2019. https://nypost.com.

Joe Sommerlad, "Pride 2019: What Happened at the Stonewall Riots and How Did They Inspire the LGBT+ Rights Movement?," *The Independent* (London), 2019. www.independent.co.uk.

Index

Note: Boldface page numbers indicate illustrations.

Picture Credits

About the Author

Hal Marcovitz is a former newspaper reporter and columnist who makes his home in Chalfont, Pennsylvania. He is the author of more than two hundred books for young readers.